AF322683

Where Has Amelia Gone To?

The Amelia Earhart Story

Biography of Famous People

Children's Women Biographies

BABY PROFESSOR

EDUCATION KIDS

Speedy Publishing LLC
40 E. Main St. #1156
Newark, DE 19711
www.speedypublishing.com

Copyright 2017

In this book, we're going to cover the exciting life and tragic death of Amelia Earhart, who was one of the first women aviators. So, let's get right to it!

WHO WAS AMELIA EARHART?

Amelia Earhart was one of the first women who obtained a pilot's license. She had several historic flights and in 1928 she was the first woman to make a flight across the Atlantic. She was also the first pilot to fly over both the Atlantic and Pacific Oceans.

Amelia Earhart

HAMMOND Y
DEPARTMENT OF COMMERCE
BUREAU OF AIR COMMERCE

Born in Atchison, Kansas on July 24, 1897, Amelia was a Midwest girl. She spent much of her youth in the home of her mother's parents. Amelia was named after her mother who was nicknamed "Amy." Her father Edwin Earhart was a smart man but he was always struggling to make money and put his family into secure circumstances. His difficulties led him to abuse alcohol.

When the family was in crisis, Amy would ship her daughters Amelia and Muriel to their home of their grandparents house. There were plenty of adventures for Amelia and her sister and they were both tomboys. They wandered around the neighborhood, climbed trees and went hunting for rats, which Amelia shot with a rifle. They liked to play football and baseball too.

When she was seven, she built a roller coaster with her sister and uncle. When she crashed, she exclaimed, "it was like flying." The first time she ever saw a real plane was at the Iowa State Fair in 1908. The plane she saw was one of the first planes built by the Wright Brothers. She was only eleven years old and, of course, she only saw the plane and didn't ride in it.

AMELIA'S CAREER PATH WAS UNCERTAIN

Amelia kept a scrapbook of famous women who had succeeded in fields dominated by men, but she still wasn't sure what she wanted to do with her life as she got into her teenage years.

Because her father hadn't been the best provider, Amelia grew up to be very independent and self-confident. After she graduated high school she wasn't sure what path she should take. She was attending Ogontz School when she decided she wanted to be a nurse's aide.

OCKH
NR
6020

She took care of wounded World War I soldiers for a while but then decided she wanted to be a mechanic. She hadn't found her calling yet. She went back to school to become a medical researcher but things soon changed in terms of the direction she would take with her life.

AMELIA'S FIRST FLIGHT

Amelia was 23 years old when she and her father attended an air show presented in California. That day she went on her first plane ride. She later stated that as soon as the plane was a few feet off the ground, she had decided that she would be a pilot. She wanted to fly!

Matson Navigation Company-Archives

Amelia Earhart - Royal, 1934

Not only did she want to get her pilot's license, she wanted to buy her own plane! With a lot of hard work and some money that she borrowed from her mother Amy, Amelia began taking flying lessons. She kept saving and saving until she had the money to purchase her own plane.

Finally the day came when she was able to buy her first airplane. It was a second-hand biplane that was painted a bright yellow, but she loved it. She nicknamed it "Canary" and she broke the world altitude record for female pilots when she flew it up to 14,000 feet.

AN IMPORTANT PHONE CALL

In April of 1928 Amelia got an unexpected phone call at work. She was busy and didn't want to answer, but the caller insisted it was important. The caller wanted to know if she would like to take an airplane ride across the Atlantic Ocean.

Once she determined that it wasn't a prank call, she said a resounding "Yes!" and her life was changed forever. Amelia had an interview with the project coordinators in New York and she also met George P. Putnam, the book publisher.

Amelia and Pilot Bill Stultz

She was the navigator on the flight, not the pilot, but Amelia must have recognized that this was just the beginning of her career as a pilot. Pilot Bill Stultz, co-pilot Slim Gordon, and Amelia landed in Wales after a 21-hour trip across the Atlantic.

She was now the first woman to have flown across the Atlantic Ocean and came back to the US as a hero. There was a parade in her honor in New York and she met President Coolidge. Today, planes routinely fly across the Atlantic Ocean in 8 hours or less.

She and George Putnam continued to see each other and in 1931 they married. Amelia didn't want her husband to dominate her and so she referred to their partnership as a marriage "with dual flight controls."

SOLO FLIGHT ACROSS THE ATLANTIC

Amelia wanted more though. She and George were working on plans to ensure her place in aviation history. She wanted to pilot her own plane in a solo flight across the Atlantic as famous aviator Charles Lindbergh had done. She planned to take the same route that Lindbergh had taken in 1927.

It was four years after her passenger ride across the Atlantic, but she was now ready to fly solo. She took off from Newfoundland in a red Lockheed Vega plane. It was May 21, 1932, the five-year anniversary of Lindbergh's flight on the day she took off.

The flight was incredibly perilous. There was stormy weather and thick clouds. Her plane's windshield and wings became covered with ice. Mechanical problems threatened her safety, but she crossed the Atlantic fourteen hours after she took off. She couldn't make it to Paris so she landed in a pasture in the Northern part of Ireland and she scared the neighborhood cows and farmers!

As the news spread, the media surrounded her in Europe as well as when she came home to the US. She was presented with a prestigious gold medal given by the National Geographic Society and offered to her by President Hoover. She also received the Distinguished Flying Cross. It was the first time this medal had ever been given to a woman. Her place in history was now assured.

SOLO FLIGHT ACROSS THE PACIFIC

For the next two years, Amelia continued to fly and she set a new altitude record at 18,415 feet that wasn't broken for years. She was ready for a new challenge and on January 11, 1935 she took off to fly solo from Honolulu across the Pacific Ocean to California.

She piloted the flight successfully and became the first aviator to accomplish that feat. During the 2,400-mile flight, she opened up a thermos with hot chocolate and drank it to warm up because the inside of the plane was so cold. When back on land, she made presentations about flying and spoke as a champion for women's rights.

FLIGHT AROUND THE WORLD

As her 40th birthday approached, Amelia was ready for an even bigger challenge. She wanted to be first woman aviator to fly around the world. She had her twin-engine Lockhead Electra rebuilt after it had been damaged that March. On June 1st of 1937, she and Fred Noonan, her navigator, left from Miami to begin the long journey of 29,000 miles.

Amelia Earhart Award

Be it known that

MARK A. KUKUCKA

HAS SATISFACTORILY COMPLETED ALL REQUIREMENTS
AND IS ENTITLED TO THE

AMELIA EARHART AWARD

GIVEN AT

NATIONAL HEADQUARTERS

CIVIL AIR PATROL

AUXILIARY OF THE UNITED STATES AIR FORCE

THIS   29th   DAY OF   October   1976

NATIONAL COMMANDER

COMMANDER, HQ CIVIL AIR PATROL-USAF

When they got to Lae in New Guinea they had already completed 22,000 miles of their trip and only had 7,000 miles to go. They found that the maps they were using for Noonan to navigate were not very accurate.

This was of particular concern on this leg of the trip since their target location for landing was Howland Island, a small island in the Pacific Ocean only half a mile wide. US ships were waiting along the path as markers including the US Coast Guard ship ITASCA, which was stationed just offshore of where they were to land.

On the morning of July 3, 1937, Amelia reported their position and indicated that the Electra was on the correct course, about 20 miles southwest of the Nukumanu Islands. At this point their fuel was running very low and they couldn't see the ITASCA.

It's thought that Noonan's map of the destination island's location was off by about five nautical miles. The ITASCA tried to signal them but it's not known if Amelia could see them or not. It was thought that their tanks had no more fuel and that they ditched or crashed at sea.

THEORIES ABOUT THE DEATH OF EARHART AND NOONAN

There were massive searches looking for the aviator and her navigator, but after many attempts, she was officially declared dead in 1939.

The search for her remains continues and in October 2014, the International Group for Historic Aircraft Recovery (TIGHAR) reported that they had identified a small piece of Earhart's plane. The fragment had been found on a small, uninhabited island in the southwestern Pacific. The legacy of Amelia Earhart still inspires aviators around the world today.

AMELIA EARHART
BORN: JULY 24, 1898
DIED: JULY 2, 1937

FLEW ATLANTIC OCEAN SOLO'
MAY 20-21, 1932

FIRST TO FLY PACIFIC OCEAN,
HONOLULU TO CALIFORNIA, SOLO
JANUARY 11-12, 1935

MOST FAMOUS AND ONE OF THE MOST
BELOVED WOMEN FLIERS IN HISTORY
OF AMERICAN AVIATION

Now you know more about Amelia Earhart and the mystery surrounding her disappearance. You can find more Biographies about Famous Women from Baby Professor by searching the website of your favorite book retailer.

Visit

BABY PROFESSOR
EDUCATION KIDS

www.BabyProfessorBooks.com
to download Free Baby Professor eBooks
and view our catalog of new and exciting
Children's Books